T0071047

Carols for SA & Men

Contents

All bells in paradise 3

Angels' Carol 14

Candlelight Carol 23

Donkey Carol 29

Love came down at Christmas 37

Mary's Lullaby 40

Star Carol 44

The Very Best Time of Year 51

What sweeter music 57

Index of Orchestrations 64

MUSIC DEPARTMENT

OXFORD
UNIVERSITY PRESS

OXFORD
UNIVERSITY PRESS

Great Clarendon Street, Oxford OX2 6DP,
United Kingdom

Oxford University Press is a department of the University of Oxford.
It furthers the University's objective of excellence in research, scholarship,
and education by publishing worldwide. Oxford is a registered trade mark of
Oxford University Press in the UK and in certain other countries

This collection © Oxford University Press 2018

John Rutter has asserted his right under the Copyright, Designs
and Patents Act, 1988, to be identified as the Composer of these Works

First published 2018

All rights reserved. No part of this publication may be reproduced,
stored in a retrieval system, or transmitted, in any form or by any means,
without the prior permission in writing of Oxford University Press

Permission to perform the works in this anthology in public
(except in the course of divine worship) should normally be obtained from
a local performing right licensing organization, unless the owner or the occupier
of the premises being used already holds a licence from such an organization.
Likewise, permission to make and exploit a recording of these works
should be obtained from a local mechanical copyright licensing organization

Enquiries concerning reproduction outside the scope of the above
should be directed to the Music Rights Department, Oxford University Press, at
music.permissions.uk@oup.com or at the address above

ISBN 978–0–19–352418–7

Music originated on Sibelius
Printed in Great Britain on acid-free paper by
Halstan & Co. Ltd, Amersham, Bucks.

All bells in paradise

*Words and music by
JOHN RUTTER

*The title line of the text is taken from the 15th-century Corpus Christi Carol.

© Collegium Music Publications 2013 and 2018. Exclusively licensed worldwide to Oxford University Press.
Photocopying this copyright material is ILLEGAL.

20
A
p e dolce
S.
sound to hear:
All bells in pa-ra-dise I heard them
A.
sound to hear:
All bells in pa-ra-dise I heard them
M.
All bells in pa-ra-dise I heard them
p
26
ring,
Sound-ing in ma-jes-ty the news that they
ring,
Sound-ing in ma-jes-ty the news that they
ring,
Sound-ing in ma-jes-ty the news that they
31
cresc.
mf
bring;
All bells in pa-ra-dise I heard them
cresc.
mf
bring;
All bells in pa-ra-dise I heard them
cresc.
mf
bring;
All bells in pa-ra-dise I heard them
cresc.
mf

36
(mf)
ring, Wel - com - ing our Sa - viour, born on
ring, Wel - com - ing our Sa - viour, born on
ring, Wel-com-ing our Sa - viour, born on
p
40
mp
earth a hea - ven - ly King. All bells in
mp
earth a hea - ven - ly King. All bells in
mp
earth a hea - ven - ly King. Ding dong,
B
f
Gt.
Gt. p cresc.
B
f
45
mf
mp
pa - ra - dise I heard them ring: 'Glo - ry to God on high' the
mf
mp
pa - ra - dise I heard them ring: 'Glo - ry to God on high' the
mf
mp
ding dong, ding dong, ding dong, 'Glo - ry to God on high' the
Sw.
mf
Sw.

50
an - gel voi - ces sing.
an - gel voi - ces sing.
an - gel voi - ces sing.
Ch.
Sw.
mp
Ch.
56
C MEN
mp dolce
2. Lost in awe and won - der, Doubt-ing, I asked what this
p
Sw.
Ped. 16' off
62
cresc.
sign might be: Christ our Mes - si - ah re-vealed in a
cresc.
(+16')

67
mf
dim.
sta - ble, A mar - vel-lous sight, a mar - vel-lous sight to
mf
dim.
72
D p e dolce
All bells in pa-ra-dise I heard them
p e dolce
All bells in pa-ra-dise I heard them
mp
p e dolce
see. All bells in pa-ra-dise I heard them
D
mp
p
77
ring, Sound - ing in ma-jes-ty the news that they
ring, Sound - ing in ma-jes-ty the news that they
ring, Sound - ing in ma-jes-ty the news that they

82
cresc.
mf
bring; All bells in pa-ra-dise I heard them
cresc.
mf
bring; All bells in pa-ra-dise I heard them
cresc.
mf
bring; All bells in pa-ra-dise I heard them
cresc.
mf

87
(mf)
ring, Wel-com-ing our Sa-viour, born on
(mf)
ring, Wel-com-ing our Sa-viour, born on
(mf)
ring, Wel-com-ing our Sa-viour, born on
p

91
mp
pp dolce e legato
E
earth a hea - ven - ly King. 3. He comes down in
earth a hea - ven - ly King. 3. He comes down in
earth a hea - ven - ly King. 3. He comes down in
Sw. p
Man.
pp
96
peace, a child in hu - mi - li - ty, The keys to his king - dom be -
peace, a child in hu - mi - li - ty, The keys to his king - dom be -
peace, a child in hu - mi - li - ty, The keys to his king - dom be -
(Choir unaccompanied)
101
cresc.
mp
p
-long to the poor; Be - fore him shall kneel the kings with their trea - sures, gold
-long to the poor; Be - fore him shall kneel the kings with their trea - sures, gold
-long to the poor; Be - fore him shall kneel the kings with their trea - sures, gold

107
poco rit.
pp
in - cense and myrrh, in - cense and myrrh.
F a tempo
mp
Ah
in - cense and myrrh, in - cense and myrrh.
in - cense and myrrh, in - cense and myrrh.
All bells in
Sw. p
Ped.
112
ah
pa - ra - dise I heard them ring,
116
Sound - ing in ma - jes - ty the news that they bring;

120
cresc.
mf
All bells in pa-ra-dise I heard them
cresc.
mf
All bells in pa-ra-dise I heard them
cresc.
mf
All bells in pa-ra-dise I heard them
cresc.
mf

124
dim.
p
ring, Ah
dim.
p
ring, Ah
dim.
mp
ring, Wel-com-ing our Sa-viour, born on
mp

128
earth a hea - ven-ly King.
Gt.
cresc.
Gt.
132
G
f
mf
All bells in pa-ra-dise I heard them ring: 'Glo - ry to
f
mf
All bells in pa-ra-dise I heard them ring: 'Glo - ry to
f
mf
Ding dong, ding dong, ding dong, ding dong, 'Glo - ry to
G
Sw.
f
mf
Sw.

137
mp
dim.
rall.
p
God on high' the an - gel voi - ces sing, The
mp
dim.
p
God on high' the an - gel voi - ces sing, The
mp
dim.
p
God on high' the an - gel voi - ces sing, The
rall.
mp
dim.
p
meno mosso
molto rit.
Lento
142
dim.
pp
an - gel voi - ces sweet - ly sing.
dim.
pp
an - gel voi - ces sweet - ly sing.
dim.
pp
an - gel voi - ces sweet - ly sing.
meno mosso
molto rit.
Lento
dim.
pp

Angels' Carol

Words and music by
JOHN RUTTER

© Oxford University Press 1988 and 2018. Photocopying this copyright material is ILLEGAL.

16
unis.
God that Christ the Lord is here?
A
19
SOPRANOS and ALTOS
mf
Have you heard the news that they bring from hea - ven
MEN
mf
Have you heard the news that they bring from hea - ven
A
23
To the hum - ble shep - herds who have wait - ed long?
To the hum - ble shep - herds who have wait - ed long?
cresc.

27
B
f joyfully
S.
Glo-ri-a in ex-cel-sis De-o, Glo-ri-a in ex-
A.
Glo-ri-a in ex-cel-sis De-o, Glo-ri-a in ex-
M.
Glo-ri-a in ex-cel-sis De-o, Glo-ri-a in ex-
f
31
mf
-cel-sis De-o! Hear the an-gels sing their joy-ful song.
-cel-sis De-o! Hear the an-gels sing their joy-ful song.
-cel-sis De-o! Hear them sing their joy-ful song.
35
C
p
Ah
p
Ah
p legato
2. He is come in peace
dim.
p legato

39
Ah
Ah
in the win-ter's still - ness, Like a gen - tle snow - fall
43
mp
Ah
He is come in
mp
Ah
He is come in
in the gen - tle night;
46
mf dolce
joy like the sun at morn - ing Fill-ing all the
mf dolce
joy like the sun at morn - ing Fill-ing all the
mp
Ah
ah
mf

50
D
dim.
world with ra - diance and with light.
dim.
world with ra - diance and with light.
p dolce
ah
He is come in
D
dim.
p
54
p
Hum
p
Hum
love as the child of Ma - ry;
In a sim - ple
58
poco cresc.
(hum)
poco cresc.
(hum)
poco cresc.
sta - ble we have seen his birth:
poco cresc.

62
E
mp
Glo-ri-a in ex-cel-sis De-o,
mp
Glo-ri-a in ex-cel-sis De-o,
mp
Glo-ri-a in ex-cel-sis De-o!
E
mp
dim.
66
p
Hear the an-gels sing-ing 'Peace on earth'.
p
Hear the an-gels sing-ing 'Peace on earth'.
p
Hear them sing 'Peace on earth'.
p
cresc.
mp cresc.
70
F
f
3. He will bring new
f
3. He will bring new light
f
3. He will bring new light
F
f
mf rhythmic
Ped.

73
light to a world in dark - ness, Like a bright star shin - ing
to a world in dark - ness, Like a bright star shin - ing
to a world in dark - ness, Like a bright star shin - ing
sim.
77
in the skies a - bove; He will bring new
in the skies a - bove;
in the skies a - bove; He will bring new
80
hope to the wait-ing na - tions When he comes to
He will bring new hope to the wait-ing na - tions
hope, he will bring new hope to the na - tions When he comes to

84
mf
G
reign in pu - ri - ty and love.
mf
f
When he comes in pu - ri - ty and love. Let the earth re -
mf
f
reign in pu - ri - ty and love.
G
Let the earth re -
mp
cresc.
mf
88
f
Let the earth re - joice at the Sa - viour's com - ing; Let the hea - vens
-joice at the Sa - viour's com - ing;
-joice at the Sa - viour's com - ing; Let the hea - vens
92
an - swer with the joy - ful morn:
Let the hea - vens an - swer with the joy - ful morn:
an - - - - - swer with the morn:
cresc.

96 H
Glo-ri-a in ex-cel-sis De-o, Glo-ri-a in ex-cel-sis De-o!
Glo-ri-a in ex-cel-sis De-o, Glo-ri-a in ex-cel-sis De-o!
Glo-ri-a in ex-cel-sis De-o, Glo-ri-a in ex-cel-sis De-o!
f
dim.
100
mf
Hear the an-gels sing-ing 'Christ is born',
dim.
rall.
Hear the an-gels sing-ing 'Christ is born',
Hear them sing-ing 'Christ is born',
104 Tranquil ♩ = 92
rall. al fine
p dolce
Hear the an-gels sing-ing 'Christ is born'.
Hum
Ped.

Candlelight Carol

Words and music by
JOHN RUTTER

*In verse 1, lower notes are for altos, in verse 2 for lower men's voices.

© Oxford University Press 1985 and 2018. Photocopying this copyright material is ILLEGAL.

A (C)
21(57)
p molto legato
cresc.
S.
Can- dle- light, an-gel light, fire-light and star-glow Shine on his
A.
Can - dle - light, an-gel light and star - glow Shine on his
M.
Can - dle - light, an-gel light and star-glow Shine on his
Play in verse 2 only – verse 1 unaccompanied
Ch.
26(62)
f
cra - dle till break - ing of dawn. Glo-ri - a, glo-ri - a
Glo-ri - a, glo-ri - a
Glo - ri - a
Play in both verses
Sw.
mf

31(67)
dim.
mp
dim.
in ex-cel - sis De - o! An - gels are sing - ing; the Christ child is
dim.
mp
dim.
in ex-cel - sis De - o! An - gels are sing - ing; the Christ child is
dim.
mp
dim.
in ex-cel - sis De - o! An - gels_ are sing - ing, Christ is
Ch.
dim.
p
36
1
B
2
p
born.
B
(Ch.)
Man.
Ped.

73
D
p
3. Find him at Beth - le - hem laid in a
3. Find him at Beth - le - hem laid in a
3. Find him at Beth - le - hem laid in a
D
78
man - ger: Christ our Re - deem - er a - sleep in the hay,
man - ger: Christ our Re - deem - er a - sleep in the hay,
man - ger: Christ our Re - deem - er a - sleep in the hay,
83
mf cresc.
f
p
God-head in - car-nate and hope of sal - va - tion: A child with his
God-head in - car-nate and hope of sal - va - tion: Hum
God-head in - car-nate and hope of sal - va - tion: Hum
Sw.
Man.

88
E
mo - ther that first Christ - mas Day.
Ah
Ah
molto dolce
Can - dle - light, an - gel light,
E
Ch.
Ped.

93
Ah
Ah
fire - light and star - glow Shine on his cra - dle till break - ing of

98
f
dim.
Glo-ri-a, glo-ri-a in ex-cel - sis De-o!
f
dim.
Glo - ri-a, glo - ri-a in ex-cel-sis De-o!
f
dim.
dawn. Glo - - ri - a in ex-cel - sis De - o!
Sw.
cresc.
f
dim.

rall.
103
mp
dim.
p
An - gels are sing - ing; the Christ child is born.
mp
dim.
p
Hum
mp
dim.
p
Hum
Ch.
rall.
p

Donkey Carol

Words and music by
JOHN RUTTER

Allegretto comodo e grazioso ♪ = *c.*184

PIANO

mf

6

SOPRANOS

mf

1. Don - key rid - ing o-ver the bum-py

dim.

mp

12

road, Car - ry Ma - ry, all with her hea-vy load;

MEN

mp

Fol - low

p

© Oxford University Press 1975 and 2018. Photocopying this copyright material is ILLEGAL.

18
SOPRANOS
mf
S.
Un - til you find a sta - ble,
mf
M.
Jo - seph, lead-ing you on your way Un - til you find a sta - ble,
mp
23
poco rall.
a tempo
mp
some-where to rest and stay. Don - key rid - ing o-ver the bum-py road,
mp
some-where to rest and stay. Don - key rid - ing o-ver the bum-py road,
poco rall.
a tempo
p
29
cresc.
mf
dim.
p
S.
Car - ry Ma - ry, all with her hea-vy, all with her hea-vy, all with her hea-vy
ALTOS
mp cresc.
mf
dim.
p
A.
Car - ry Ma - ry, all, all, all with her
cresc.
mf
dim.
p
M.
Car - ry Ma - ry, all with her hea-vy, all with her hea-vy, all with her hea-vy
cresc.
mf
dim.
p

35
load.
load.
mf
2. Don - key
mf
mp
40
watch - ing o-ver the Je-sus child, See the ba - by
45
SOPRANOS and ALTOS
mf
all with his mo-ther mild; Hear the an - gels sing-ing their song on
50
high: 'No-well, no - well, no - well', their ca - rol - ling fills the
mf

54
poco rall.
a tempo
unis.
S. and A.
S.
A.
sky.
Don - key watch - ing o-ver the Je-sus child,
mf
M.
Don - key watch - ing o-ver the Je-sus child,
poco rall.
a tempo
mp
59
mp cresc.
mf
dim.
p
See the ba - by, all with his mo-ther, all with his mo-ther, all with his mo-ther
See the ba - by, all, all, all with his mo-ther
See the ba - by, all with his mo-ther, all with his mo-ther, all with his mo-ther
cresc.
65
(S. and A.)
p dolce e legato
mild.
3. Don - key rest - ing all in a man-ger stall,
mild.
una corda

71
With the ox - en wor-ship the Lord of all. Hush, he
MEN pp
Hush,
76
mp
lies a - sleep on his bed of hay While Ma-ry sings so sweet - ly
mp
he lies While Ma-ry sings so sweet - ly
mp
81
p
'Lul - la, lul-la - lay'. Don - key rest - ing all in a man-ger
p
'Lul - la, lul- la, lul-la, lul-la - lay'. rest - ing all in a man-ger
p
'Lul - la, lul-la, lul - la - lay'.
p

86
S.
stall, With the ox - en wor-ship the Lord, wor-ship the Lord,
A.
stall, With the ox - en wor - ship, wor-ship the Lord,
91
poco rit.
accel.
Tempo I
f
wor-ship the Lord of all.
No-well, no-well, no-well, no-
f
wor-ship the Lord of all.
No-well, no-well, no-well, no-
M.
f
4. Don - key skip for
poco rit.
accel.
Tempo I
mp cresc.
f
tre corde
97
S.
A.
-well, no-well, no - well, no-well, no - well, no-well, no-well, no-well, no-well, no-
M.
joy as you go your way; Al - le - lu - ia, Je-sus is born to-

102
-well, no - well. Hark, the bells ring out with their mes-sage
- day. Hark, the bells ring out with their mes-sage
106
cresc.
ff
clear: Re-joice and sing that Christ our Sa-viour di-vine is here.
cresc.
ff
clear: Re-joice and sing that Christ our Sa-viour di-vine is here.
cresc.
ff
111
f
mf
cresc.
No-well, no-well, no-well, no-well, no-well, no-well, no-well, no-well, Al-le-
f
mf
cresc.
Don - key skip for joy as you go your way, Al - le -
f
mf
cresc.

116
rallentando
S.
-lu - ia, al - le-lu-ia, al - le-lu-ia, al - le - lu - ia, Christ is
A.
-lu - ia, al - le-lu-ia, al - le-lu-ia, al - le - lu - ia, Christ is
M.
-lu - ia, al - le-lu-ia, al - le - lu - ia, Christ is
rallentando
122
ten.
a tempo
rall. al fine
born to - day.
born to - day.
born to - day.
a tempo
rall. al fine

Love came down at Christmas

Words by
Christina Rossetti (1830–94)

JOHN RUTTER

© Oxford University Press 1971 and 2018. Photocopying this copyright material is ILLEGAL.

14
S.
A.
p
Ah
ah
MEN
mp dolce cantabile
M.
2. Wor - ship we the God - head, Love in - car - nate, Love di - vine;
mp
Ped.
19
cresc.
mf
ah
But where-with for sa - cred sign?
Wor - ship we our Je - sus:
mf
cresc.
mf
Man.
23
mp
But where-with for sa - - cred sign?
mp
mp
Ped.

27
p
3. Love shall be our to - ken, Love be yours and love be mine;
p
to - - ken,
p
31
cresc.
mf
Love to God and all men, Love for plea and gift and sign;
cresc.
mf
Love to God and all men,
35
p
poco rit.
Love for plea and gift and sign.
p
poco rit.
p
pp

Mary's Lullaby

Words and music by
JOHN RUTTER

Andante tranquillo ♩ = *c.* 69

PIANO or ORGAN

p legato sempre

(Ped.)

5(23)

SOPRANOS

S.

p 1. See the child that Ma - ry bore On her lap so soft - ly
mf 2. Flights of an - gels round his head Sing him joy - ful hymns of

ALTOS

A.

p 1. See the child that Ma - ry bore On her lap so soft - ly
mf 2. Flights of an - gels round his head Sing him joy - ful hymns of

(Man.)

8(26)

sleep - ing: In a sta - ble cold and poor, Ox and
greet - ing: *p* 'Peace on earth, good-will to men,' Each to

sleep - ing: In a sta - ble cold and poor, Ox and
greet - ing: *p* 'Peace on earth, good-will to men,' Each to

© Oxford University Press 1979 and 2018. Photocopying this copyright material is ILLEGAL.

11(29)
p
ass their vi - gil keep - ing.
each the song re - peat - ing.
Sing lul - la - by, sing lul - la - by, my
p
ass their vi - gil keep - ing.
each the song re - peat - ing.
Sing lul - la - by, sing lul - la - by, my
MEN p
Sing lul - la - by, my
15(33)
own dear son, my child; Lul - la - by, sing lul - la - by;
own son, my child; Lul - la - by, sing lul - la - by;
own, my child; Lul - la - by, lul - la - by;
(Man.)
19(37)
pp
1.
Lul - la - by, my lit - tle ba - by.
pp
Hum
pp
Hum
1.
pp
p
(Ped.)
(Man.)

38
ba - by.
mp cantabile
3. Shep-herds kneel-ing by his bed Of-fer
(Man.)
(Ped.)
43
ALTOS mp cantabile
A.
Bring him
M.
hom - age with-out mea - sure;
Wise men, by a bright star led,
Bring him
47
S.
pp
Sing lul - la - by, sing lul - la - by, my
A.
pp
gifts of rich-est trea - sure. Sing lul - la - by, sing lul - la - by, my
M.
pp
gifts of rich-est trea - sure. Sing lul - la - by, my
pp

51
poco cresc.
p
own dear son, my child; Lul - la - by, sing lul - la - by;
poco cresc.
p
own son, my child; Lul - la - by, sing lul - la - by;
poco cresc.
p
own, my child; Lul - la - by, lul - la - by;
poco cresc.
p
(Man.)
rall.
55
pp
Lul-la-by, my lit-tle ba - by.
pp
Hum
pp
Hum
rall.
pp
p
espress.
pp
(Ped.)

Star Carol

Words and music by
JOHN RUTTER

© Oxford University Press 1972 and 2018. Photocopying this copyright material is ILLEGAL.

*Children and/or audience may join in the melody of the refrain, which can be taught at the time of performance.

21(42)
mf lightly
Hur-ry to Beth - le-hem and see the son of Ma - ry.
mf lightly
mf
2nd time only
p
24
B
1.
mf
tr
2.
p dolce
47
C
SOLO VOICE or SEMI-CHORUS
p dolce e legato
3. See, he lies in his mo-ther's ten-der keep - ing; Je - sus Christ in her
p dolce e legato
S.
A.
Ah (or hum)
M.
p dolce e legato
C

50
lov-ing arms a-sleep. Shep-herds poor, come to wor-ship and a - dore_ him,
53
Of-fer their hum-ble gifts_ be-fore the son of Ma - ry.
p
57
D
p legato
See his star shin-ing bright In the_ sky this_ Christ-mas Night!_ Fol-low me_
p legato
D

62
joy - ful - ly; Hur-ry to Beth - le - hem and see the son of Ma - ry!
mf
66
E
f
4. Let us all pay our hom-age at the man - ger,
E
f
f
70
Sing his praise on this joy - ful Christ-mas Night; Christ is come, bring-ing

73
mf
pro-mise of sal - va - tion; Hur-ry to Beth - le - hem and see the son of
mf
mf
76
F
f
Ma - ry!
See his star shin- ing bright
f
F
cresc.
f
Ped.
sim.
80
In the sky this Christ-mas Night!
Fol - low me joy - ful - ly;

84
G
mf
cresc.
Hur-ry to Beth - le - hem and see the son of Ma - ry,
mf
cresc.
G
mf
cresc.
Poco largamente
rall.
CHILDREN/AUDIENCE (opt.)
87
f
cresc.
ff
Hur-ry to Beth - le - hem and see the son of Ma - ry!
f
cresc.
ff
Hur-ry to Beth - le - hem and see the son of Ma - ry!
f
cresc.
ff
Poco largamente
rall.
f
cresc.
ff
8va
8vb

The Very Best Time of Year

Words and music by
JOHN RUTTER

© Oxford University Press 1985 and 2018. Photocopying this copyright material is ILLEGAL.

12
SOPRANOS and ALTOS
A
mf
glow; Sounds of hap-py chil-dren's voi-ces Sing-ing ca-rols that you love to
MEN
mp
mf
Sounds of hap-py chil-dren's voi-ces Sing-ing ca-rols that you love to
A
mf
16
p
unis.
hear; Then the si-lence of the night And the win-ter air so still and clear.
p
hear; Then the si-lence of the night And the win-ter air so still and clear.
p
cresc.
20
B SOPRANOS and ALTOS
mp
Feels like you could reach and touch the sky, Or
p

23
catch a star and fly a - way;
p dolce
Feels like you could wish for
p
26
peace on earth, And all at once it would come, some day.
Ped.
29
C
mp
mf
Fa - mi - lies and friends to - geth - er Feel a spe - cial kind of love and
mp
mf
Fa - mi - lies and friends to - geth - er Feel a spe - cial kind of love and
mp
mf
Fa - mi - lies and friends to - geth - er Feel a spe - cial kind of love and
C
mp
cresc.
mf

32
mp
p
cheer, Shar-ing all the joys of Christ-mas time – The ve - ry best
cheer, Shar-ing all the joys of Christ-mas time – The ve - ry best
cheer, Shar-ing all the joys of Christ-mas time – The ve - ry best
mp
p
36
D
time of year.
time of year.
time of year.
D
mp dolce espress.
40

44
rit.
a tempo
p
cresc.
Ped.
48
E
mf warmly
Fa-mi-lies and friends to-geth-er Feel a spe-cial kind of love and
mf warmly
Fa-mi-lies and friends to-geth-er Feel a spe-cial kind of love and
mf warmly
Fa-mi-lies and friends to-geth-er Feel a spe-cial kind of love and
E
mf
51
mp
cheer, Shar-ing all the joys of Christ-mas time – The
mp
cheer, Shar-ing all the joys of Christ-mas time The
cheer, Shar-ing all the joys of Christ-mas time –
mp

54
ve - ry best time, That
ve - ry best time, That
That strange, en - chant - ed time, That
p
Ped. Ped. sim.

58
Slower till the end
dim.
pp
shin - ing, ma - gic time of year.
shin - ing, ma - gic time of year, of year.
shin - ing, ma - gic time of year, of year.
Slower till the end
Ped.

What sweeter music

Words by
Robert Herrick
(1591–1674)

JOHN RUTTER

*Slightly abridged and altered

© Oxford University Press 1988 and 2018. Photocopying this copyright material is ILLEGAL.

13
ALTOS mp
poco meno mosso
And give the ho - nour to this day That sees De-
night, fly hence a - way, And give the ho - nour to this day That sees De-
poco meno mosso
17
poco rit.
a tempo
♩ = 66
S.
pp
That sees De - cem - ber turn'd to May.
A.
dim.
pp
-cem - ber turn'd to May, That sees De - cem - ber turn'd to May.
M.
dim.
pp
mp
-cem - ber turn'd to May, That sees De - cem - ber turn'd to May. Why does the
poco rit.
a tempo
♩ = 66
dim.
p
mp
21
M.
chill - ing win-ter's morn Smile, like a field be - set with corn? Or smell like a
Ped.

25
mf
Thus on the sud - den? Come and see The cause, why
mf
mea-dow new-ly shorn Thus on the sud - den? Come and see The cause, why
mf
mp
29
mp
mf
div.
'Tis he is born, whose quick-'ning birth Gives life and
mp
mf
things thus frag-rant be: 'Tis he is born, whose quick-'ning birth Gives life and
things thus frag-rant be:
Fl.
Man.

33
S.
mp
p molto legato
unis.
lu - stre, pub-lic mirth, To hea-ven and the un-der-earth. We see him
A.
mp
p molto legato
lu - stre, pub-lic mirth, To hea-ven and the un-der-earth. We see him
M.
p molto legato
We see him
p
(Man.)

37
3
come, and know him ours, Who, with his sun - shine and his show'rs, Turns all the
3
come, and know him ours, Who, with his sun - shine and his show'rs, Turns the
3
come, and know him ours, Who, with his sun - shine and his show'rs, Turns the
(Organ tacet)

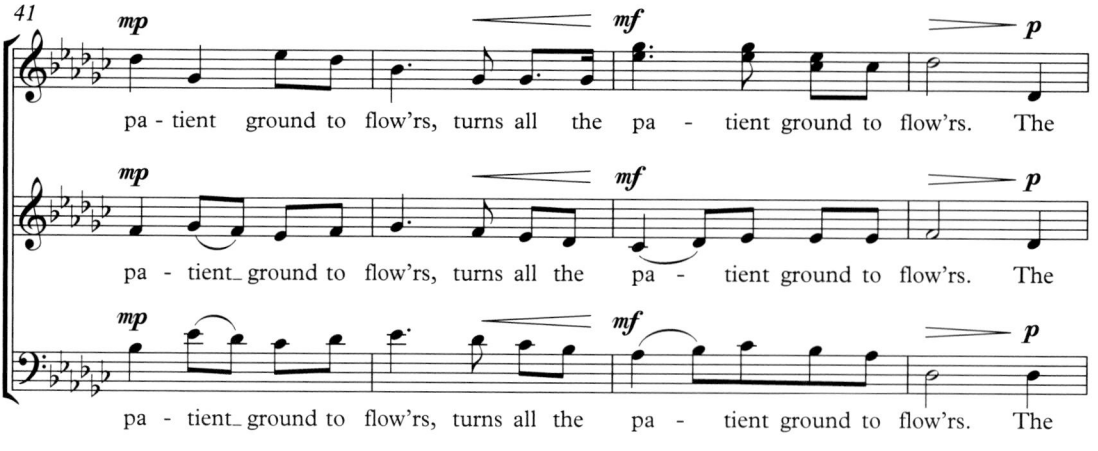
41
mp
mf
p
pa - tient ground to flow'rs, turns all the pa - tient ground to flow'rs. The
mp
mf
p
pa - tient ground to flow'rs, turns all the pa - tient ground to flow'rs. The
mp
mf
p
pa - tient ground to flow'rs, turns all the pa - tient ground to flow'rs. The

45
div.
dar-ling of the world is come, And fit it is, we find a room To
dar-ling of the world is come, And fit it is, we find a room To
dar - ling of the world is come, we
49
unis.
mp
cresc.
wel-come him, to wel-come him. The no-bler part here, is the
mf
wel-come him, to wel-come him. is the
mp
cresc.
wel - come, wel-come him. The no-bler part of all the house here, is the
pp
Man.
mp
Ped.
cresc.
53
mf > mp
3
heart, Which we will give him; and be-queath This hol - ly, and this
> mp
heart, Which we will give him; and be - queath This hol - ly, and this
mf > mp
heart,
> p
Man.

57
mf
poco f
i - vy wreath,
And Lord of all this re-vel-
mf
poco f
i - vy wreath, To do him ho-nour; who's our King, And Lord of all this re-vel-
mp
mf
poco f
To do him ho-nour; who's our King, And Lord of all this re-vel-
mp
Ped.

61
mf
p
pp molto dolce
-ling.
What sweet-er mu - sic can we bring
Than a
mf
p
pp molto dolce
-ling.
What sweet-er mu - sic can we bring
Than a
mf
p
pp molto dolce
-ling.
What sweet-er mu - sic can we bring
Than a
pp molto dolce
(Ped.)

66
poco rit.
poco meno mosso
mp
p
ca - rol, for to sing The birth of this our heav'n-ly King, the birth of
ca - rol, for to sing The birth of this our heav'n-ly King, the birth of
ca - rol, for to sing The birth of this our heav'n-ly King.
poco rit.
poco meno mosso
70
rit.
a tempo
rit.
dim.
pp
this our hea - ven - ly King.
our hea - ven - ly King.
our hea - ven - ly King.
(Ped.)

Index of Orchestrations

The following accompanied items are available in versions with orchestra. Full scores and instrumental parts are available on rental from the Oxford University Press Hire Library or appointed agent, and also on sale, where indicated.

All bells in paradise: 2fl, ob, 2cl, bsn, 2hn, hp, str

Angels' Carol: 2fl, ob, 2cl, bsn, 2hn, hp, str
Full score on sale (ISBN 978-0-19-351221-4)
Set of parts on sale (ISBN 978-0-19-351222-1)

Candlelight Carol: fl, ob, hp, str
Full score on sale (ISBN 978-0-19-341055-8)
Set of parts on sale (ISBN 978-0-19-341056-5)

Donkey Carol: 2fl, 2ob, 2cl, bsn, 2hn, glock, timp, hp, str
Full score on sale (ISBN 978-0-19-385781-0)
Set of parts on sale (ISBN 978-0-19-385782-7)
Also available with brass accompaniment: 4tpt, 3tbn, tba, perc

Mary's Lullaby: fl, ob, hp, str
Full score on sale (ISBN 978-0-19-385885-5)
Set of parts on sale (individual parts available separately)

Star Carol: 2fl, 2ob, 2cl, 2bsn, 2hn, 2perc, hp, str
Full score on sale (ISBN 978-0-19-385704-9)
Set of parts on sale (ISBN 978-0-19-385705-6)
Also available with brass accompaniment: 4tpt, 3tbn, tuba, timp, perc, pno or org

The Very Best Time of Year: fl, ob, hp, str
Full score on sale (ISBN 978-0-19-351257-3)
Set of parts on sale (ISBN 978-0-19-351258-0)

What sweeter music: accompaniment for strings
Full score on sale (ISBN 978-0-19-386010-0)
Set of parts on sale (individual parts available separately)